*everything i write has a synergistic effect
with simultaneous presence in words and lines.*

imprint/
© 2015 wilhelm singer
ISBN 978-3-7386-1028-4
publisher/ bod _ books on demand
contact/ info@wilhelmsinger.com
www.wilhelmsinger.com

in the rhythm of marta chiccovsky's and alfred lenicek's reality

i can't really consider that as a genealogical tree, but i found a "drucksache: direktor alfred lenicek dessau bauhaus" enclosed in an antique photograph at the cheng & co. antique store defensa 832 buenos aires in 2013.
history approached! the shop transformed in a vessel—in a time machine with a master.
he was talking queer...yet this world was not so closed as it seemed.

in the background: the lost reality.
"¡buenos días!"
a man greets a woman.
they resemble each other in appearance.

"le doy mis gracias mas expresivas."
the man received the response.
"muchas gracias por esperar," she said into my restored awareness.

back on the street: alfred lenicek, director of bauhaus?
an astronomical hypothesis, i thought.
in the shadow of the curtain—the corner arranged to work artistic, i started my historical investigation.
who are you, mr. alfred lenicek?

legitimation or identification

the general notion behind this story is: on a thursday evening in june 1893, alfred lenicek was born in brno, today the czech republic, as a son of a textile industry pioneer, and his later wife marta chiccovsky was born on a monday morning in august 1899 in amsterdam, the netherlands.
her family had to leave portugal generations ago.

on a thursday in 1919, her voice changed a lot.
witty, funny, and absurd.
but then she focused on the bond—a contractual bond
commanded by god, in which a man and a woman come
together to create a relationship in which god is directly
involved. they got married at the leopoldstädter tempel*,
the largest synagogue of vienna.
*leopoldstädter tempel, built in 1858 in the moorish style according to the
plans of architect leopold förster, all but the foundation was completely
destroyed by national socialist barbarians on the so-called "night of
broken glass", on 10 november 1938)

he asked her: where have you been? everywhere, and i watched
everything!

alfred lenicek died on a monday in march 1968 in new york. his
remains are buried at long island national cemetery in wellwood
avenue, farmingdale, suffolk, long island, new york.

we have to pause the file at this point. we won't fill the gap—the
despair of the year 1938. there will never be a vindication for his
loss.

the poetry of idealism

the poetry began in amsterdam*, on a balmy summer afternoon
in 1918.
Strange—now, to think of love. history tells us the first world
war was not over yet and amsterdam was situated under
gathering clouds of a flu pandemic; the government proved
unable to deal with the manifold problems of refugees.
*during world war I, the netherlands remained neutral

alfred lenicek, finally, was one of 300,000 jews serving in the
k.u.k armee*—one of the faithful servants of the crown.
*it was the first time that jews were forced into a compulsory military
service at the beginning of june 1918, his division (k.u.k. 35th infantry
division) was deployed on the western front close to st. mihiel.

but he never reached st. mihiel.
as per one of his comrades, he got sick and lost. all we know
is that, on a balmy summer afternoon in 1918, he met marta
chiccovsky in amsterdam.

living with a paradox

we should also note that i am still in buenos aires, in the shadow
of the curtain—the corner arranged to work artistic, and i
historicize the categories of the fields of conceptual disputes.

the communion starts happening on my way to new york and
later on in my "room with no view"—a reminiscence about
dimension and time.
i am unhinged with the prisoners of my story—the dictation
of my mind.
a claim to such a narrative, of course, suggests a specific idea
of time and guides the way in which i understand reality.

sunflower existence

back to the avatars of my story: marta chiccovsky and
alfred lenicek, after they fell in love in amsterdam, moved
to vienna. alfred's father provided a small business in
leopoldstadt, pillersdorfergasse, connected with his textile
work in brno.
alfred became a respected fabric designer. his reputation
reached walter gropius and, in 1925, they met in person in
dessau, germany.
in 1926, marta chiccovsky and alfred lenicek moved to dessau
and their entire purpose of life developed to a short epilogue
of bauhaus history.

the meaning of pain

it is now clear that what marta and alfred were witnessing was the implosion of humanity—in fact, a systematic genocide. 1932: the national socialists came into power in dessau, marta and alfred settled down in vienna, but it was not easy to breathe in the city known for its waltzes and sweets. in a tragic work, fate makes itself felt better, but on 9/10th november 1938, by looking in the faces of the austrian authorities and their not intervening, alfred lost his belief and his wife marta.
the word "hope" lost its meaning in the characterized evidence that moral existential thoughts are classified to be the absurd.

closing remarks

it is hard to imagine something as entrenched in human history—choreographed by creeps. the artwork is not complex in all its realities; more precisely, it completes lived experiences in stories told or untold by individuals, witnesses of the story behind the plot.
the curves of time are real in their contact with the wall. the visible expressions uncover the historical connection of the space.

early drawings

about 1900 alfred, seven years old and on vaccation with his parents, used a collection of the popular magazin "gartenlaube" to work on overpaintings.

a contemporary document

Die Gartenlaube

Illustriertes Familienblatt

Jahrgang 1900.

Verlag von Ernst Keil's Nachfolger G. m. b. H. in Leipzig.

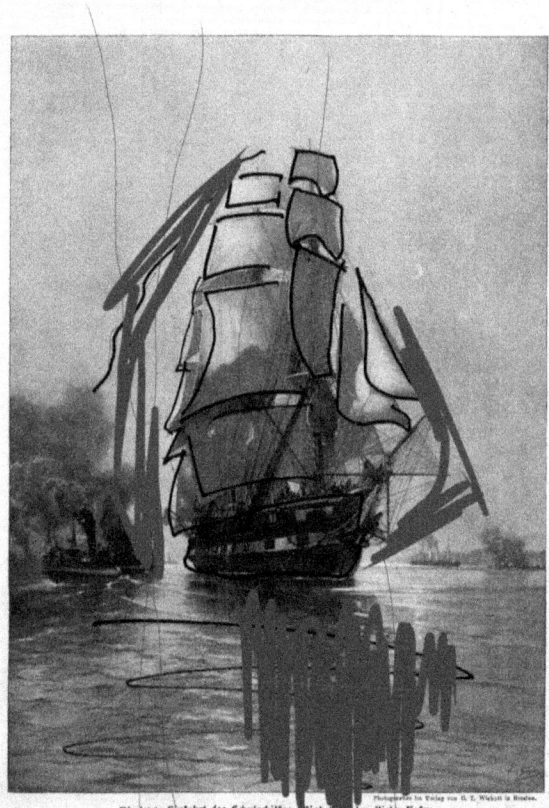

Die letzte Einfahrt des Schulschiffes „Niobe" in den Kieler Hafen.
Nach dem Gemälde von Hans Bohrdt.

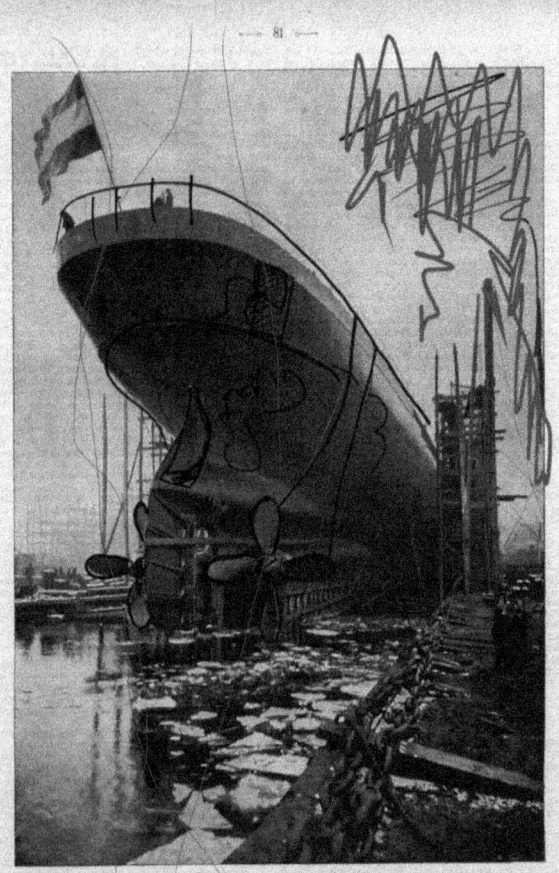

Der Schnelldampfer „Deutschland" vor dem Stapellauf.
Nach einer Aufnahme des Hofphotographen R. Matthaey. Verlag von A. Schuster in Stettin.

Die Gartenlaube

N⁰ 8. **1900.**

Illustriertes Familienblatt. — Begründet von Ernst Keil 1853.

Preis des Jahrgangs: 7 M. Zu beziehen in Wochennummern vierteljährlich 1 M. 75 Pf., oder in 28 Halbheften zu 25 Pf., oder in 14 Heften zu 50 Pf.

Im Wasserwinkel.

(2. Fortsetzung.)   Roman von W. Heimburg.

Nachdruck verboten.
Alle Rechte vorbehalten.

Eva findet keinen Augenblick Ruhe in der Nacht. Die Mutter ist wenige Zeit nach ihr heimgekommen mit verstörtem Gesicht und hat sie kurz gefragt: „Du willst also Moritz Baldorf nicht?"

„Nein, Mama, ich will ihn nicht."

Kein Wort ist weiter gewechselt worden, geschlafen haben beide nicht. In aller Morgenfrühe erst sinkt auf die wilden, heißgeweinten Reden Evas ein kurzer, unruhiger Schlummer. Fräulein Röschen Kastenstein, die die großen Arbeiten im Hause verrichtet, seit früher Morgenstunde thätig.

Frau Doktor steht auf, und nachdem sie eilig eine Tasse Kaffee getrunken hat, sagt sie zu der Frau: „Sei'n Sie leise, Frau Klinke, Fräulein schläft noch, sie ist nicht ganz wohl — achten Sie gut auf die Thür, ich gehe mal zu meinem Sohn."

Ganz aufgeregt kommt sie dort an und findet den jungen Arzt beim Kaffee in dem hübschen Eßzimmer. Die Schwiegertochter schläft noch, Robert hat ja bis halb zehn Uhr Sprechstunde, dann geht er auf Praxis, und so sie den eiligen Frühstück zugegen ist oder nicht, was thut's — es liegt so fern in den Federn, draußen bei der Mutter hat er es nie ge-

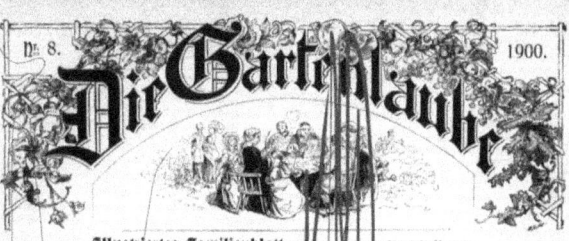

Ein Fastnachtsidyll.
Nach dem Gemälde von E. Luppe.

habt. Mama ist schlechter Laune, der Kaffee miserabel und die Butter hat Haselflecken, man hat sie nicht im Keller gehabt. Das Brot hat auch braune Flecken; bei seiner Mutter daheim war alles tadellos trotz des knappen Auskommens, die Schwiegermutter aber behauptet, ein Kaffeetrinken müsse drei Wochen aushalten, Wäsche sei kostspielig.

„Serrie, Mama, du schon? Ist denn was geschehen? — Ist Eva wieder cloud?"

Sie setzt sich zu ihm an den Tisch; trotz ihrer Kümmernis erinnert sie die Fleck wohl und besteht ihrer verschlossenen Augen darauf. „Ja, es ist um Eva," sagt sie heiser, „sie ist so wunderlich — gestern abend hat Moritz Baldorf ihr einen Antrag gemacht, und sie hat abgelehnt —."

„Die ist ja wohl rein des Deubels," führt er hervor, „da werde ich mal kommen und Deutsch mit ihr reden!"

„Nein, nein, dränge sie nur nicht," bittet die Mutter, „denn wenn sie später unglücklich werden sollte —"

„Unglücklich? Warum denn? Er ist doch ein anständiger Kerl, ein bischen Original zwar und grad kein Krösus, er riecht ein wenig nach Pferdestall und dergleichen, oder dafür ist er auch ein tüchtiger Ökonom — — J, laß mich doch machen, Mutter, ich werde ihr die Sache schon richtig vorstellen."

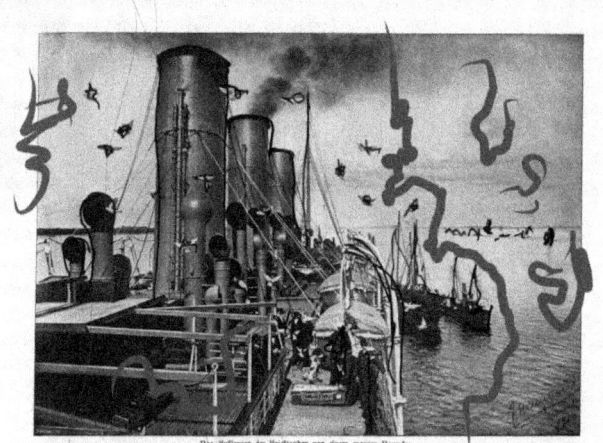

Das Auflassen der Brieftauben von einem großen Dampfer.
Nach einer photographischen Aufnahme von J. Hamann in Hamburg.

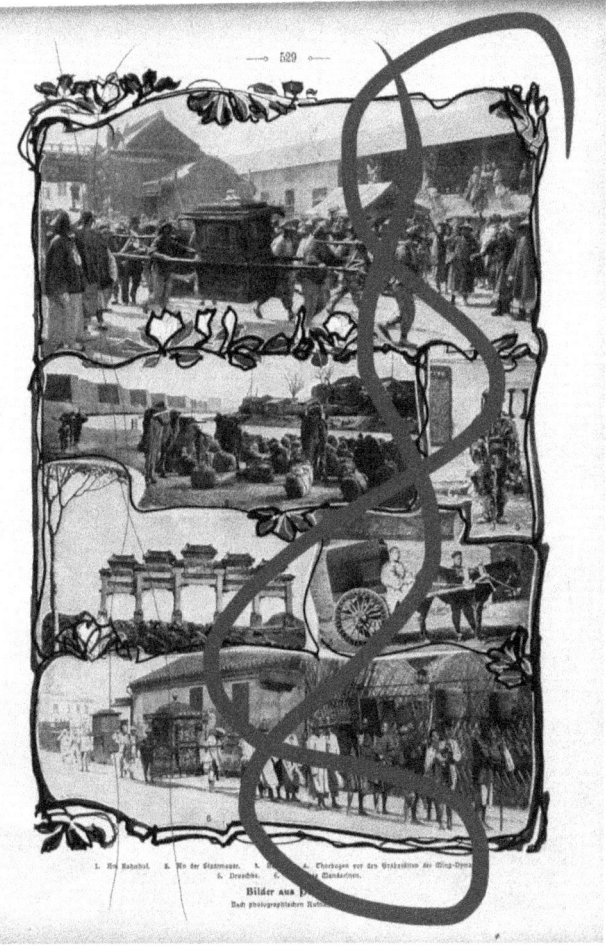

1. Am Bahnhof. 2. An der Stadtmauer. 4. Thorbogen vor den Grabstätten der Ming-Dynastie.
5. Droschke. 6. Mandarinen.
Bilder aus P
Nach photographischen Auf

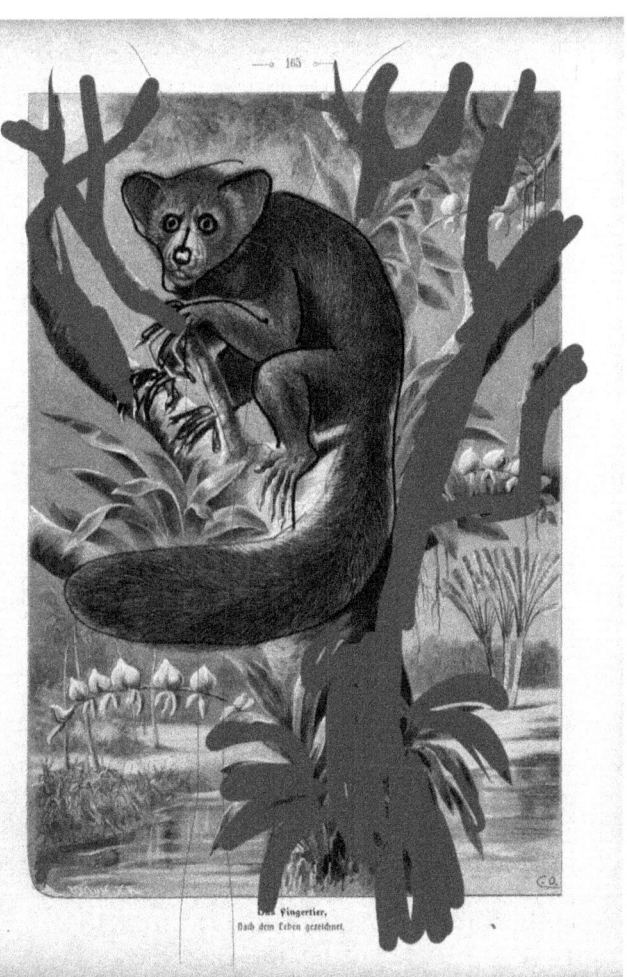

Das Fingertier.
Nach dem Leben gezeichnet.

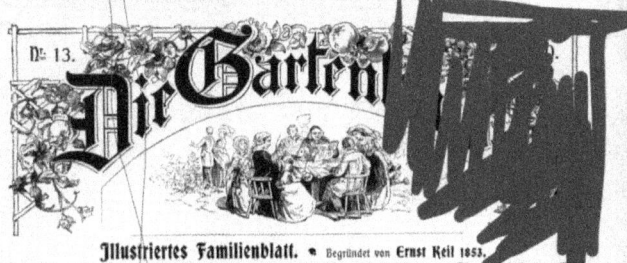

Illustriertes Familienblatt. Begründet von Ernst Keil 1853.

Preis des Jahrgangs: 7 M. Zu beziehen in Wochennummern vierteljährlich 1 M. 75 Pf., auch in 28 Halbheften zu 25 Pf. oder in 14 Heften zu 50 Pf.

Im Wasserwinkel.

Roman von W. Heimburg.

(12. Fortsetzung.)

Madame besteht darauf, Eva bis an die Hans zu fahren, „daß, wenn Dore etwa nicht daheim sein sollte, du nicht auf der Straße stehen mußt!" Eva will durchaus nicht darauf eingehen, mit in den „Winkel" zu kommen. „Laß mich, Tante, du hast ja zu Hauf deine Pflege." Nun steigt sie vor ihrer Wohnung aus und reicht Madame die Hand nochmal in den Wagen hinein. „Dore ist daheim, ich höre sie, Tante. Leb' wohl!"

Dore kommt beim Oeffnen der Haustühr sogleich gestürzt; sie glaubt, ihr Fräulein wolle sie kurz besuchen, und jammert fürchtbar, daß sie nun g'rad' mal in der Stube keinen Staub gewischt habe. „Und, Fräulein Eva, sehen Sie sich derweil ein bißchen in meine Stube, ich koch' gleich Kaffee. — Sie wohl besorgungen?"

„Nein, Dore, ich bleibe nun wieder hier," antwortet „und ich helfe dir gleich."

„Ganz? Für immer, Fräulein Eva?"

„Freilich, Dore, und das Erste ist, daß die Kinder erfahren, ich bin wieder da. Sie haben schon allzulange Ferien gehabt. Sie sagt das ein bißchen forcirt munter. „Ich gehe jetzt mal durch die Stuben, Dore, unterdes ist der Kaffee fertig, dann — vielleicht ist's am besten, ich lasse es im Wochenblatt bekannt machen, daß die Schule wieder anfängt. Wenn

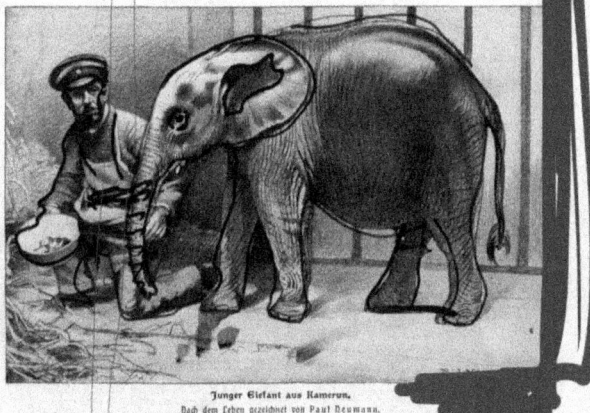

Junger Elefant aus Kamerun.
Nach dem Leben gezeichnet von Paul Neumann.

fully decoded space

a reminiscence about love, space and time in a 25 square meter room provided for daily adventures.

an excursus in empirical substantiation

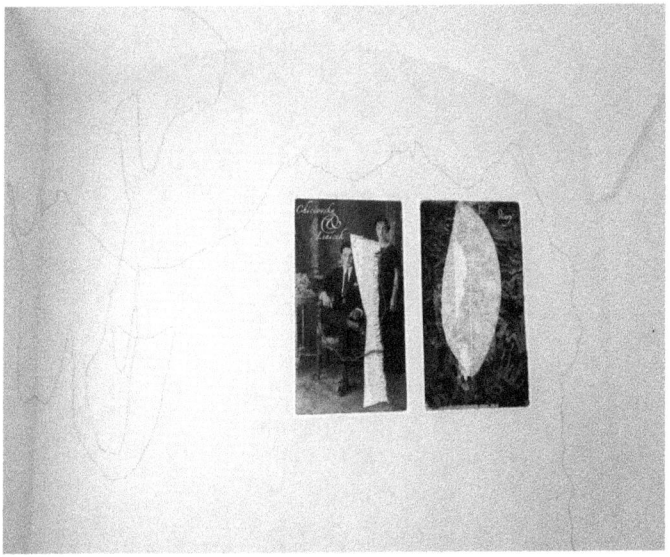

outline: pasted thread
collages: tape on antique book covers
prints: fine art prints/paper: hahnemühle william turner
environmental collages: pasted thread, old frame, textile, polaroid

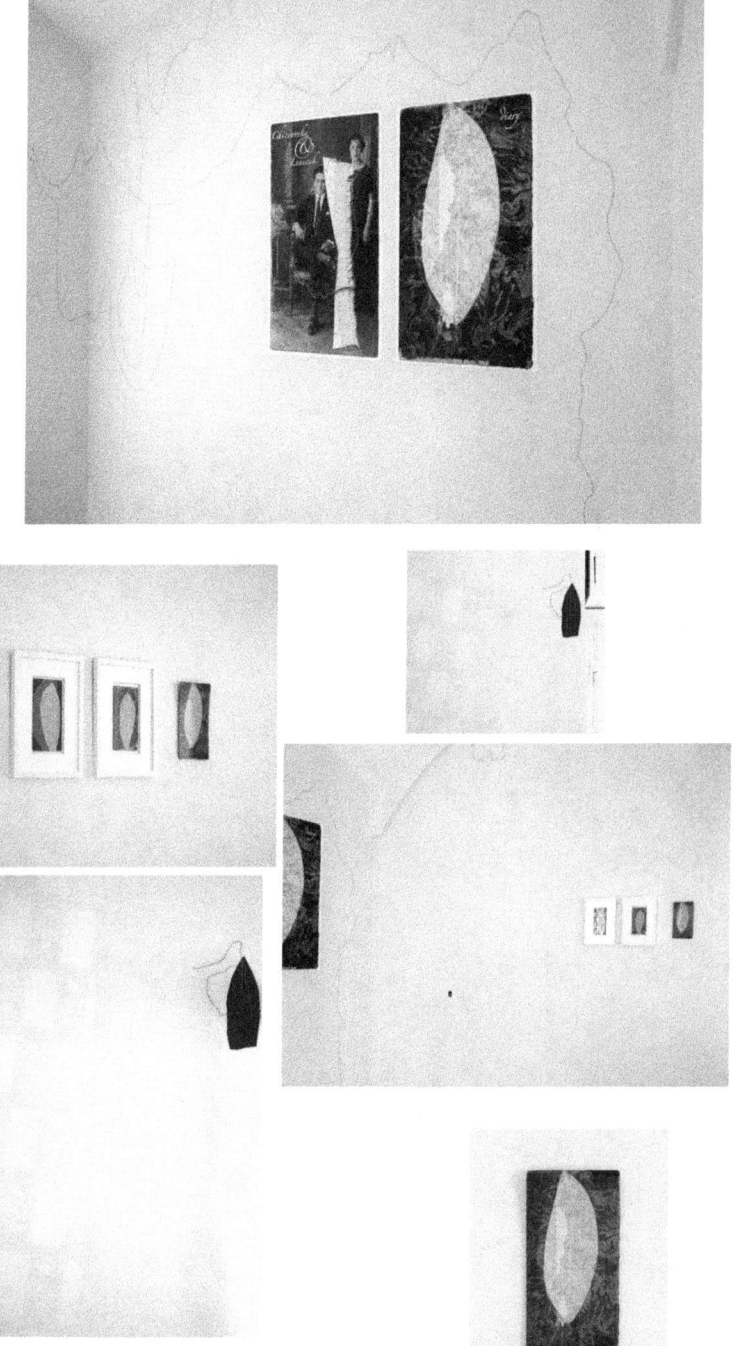

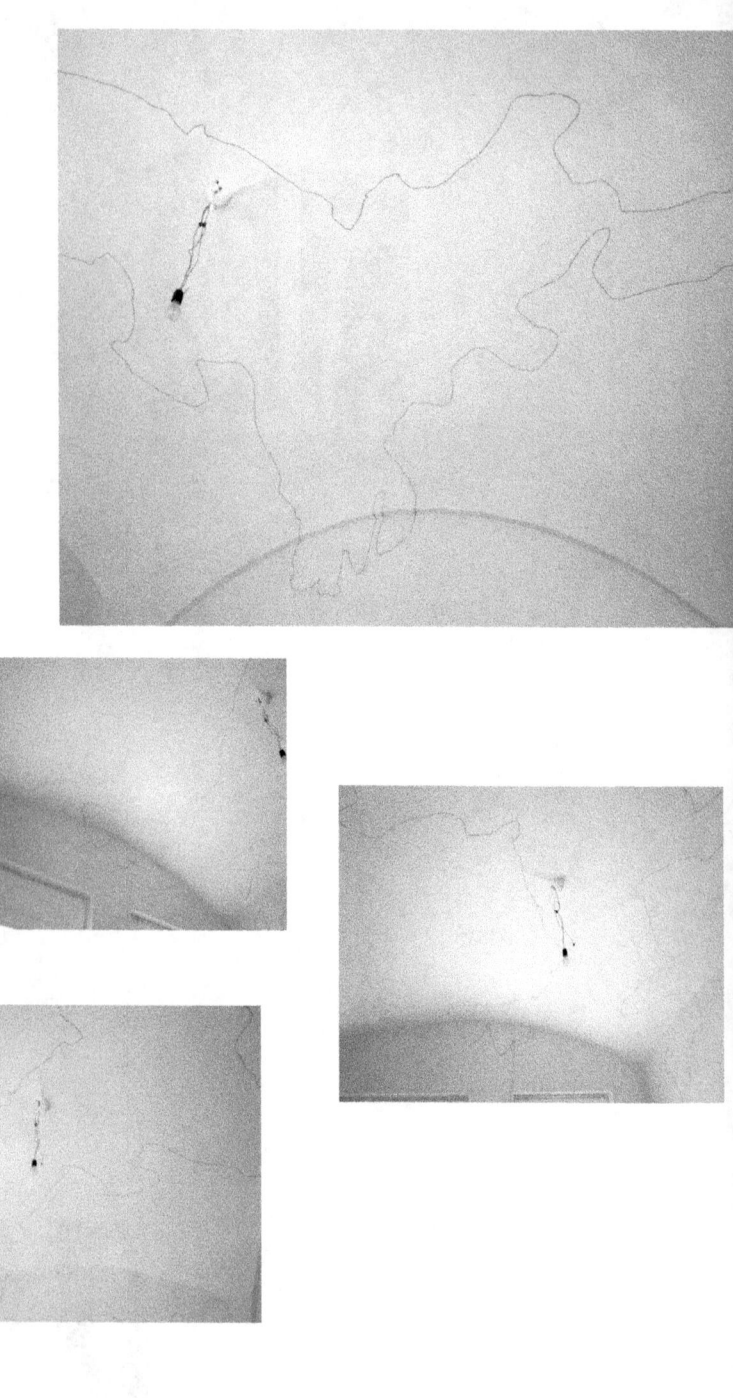

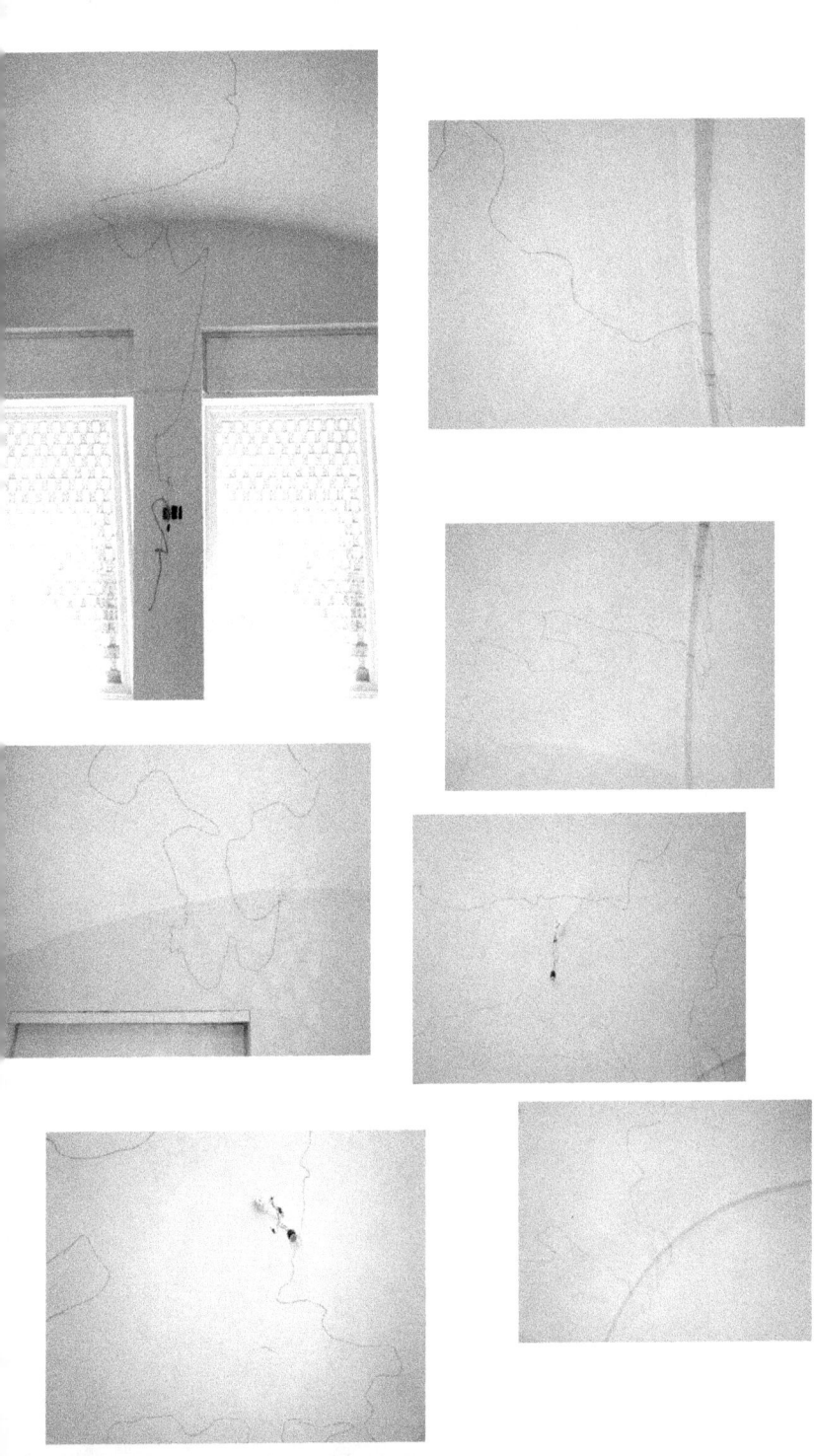

www.ingramcontent.com/pod-product-compliance
Lightning Source LLC
Chambersburg PA
CBHW050254230526
45470CB00005B/2255